LET'S FIND OUT ABOUT THE FAMILY

LET'S FIND OUT ABOUT The Family

by Valerie Pitt

Illustrated by Gloria Kamen

FRANKLIN WATTS, INC.
845 Third Avenue
New York, New York 10022

SBN 531-00065-6
Library of Congress Catalog Card Number: 78-117180
© Copyright 1970 by Franklin Watts, Inc.
Printed in the United States of America

LET'S FIND OUT ABOUT THE FAMILY

Have you ever watched a tiny baby?
He is really quite helpless.
He needs someone to wash him and feed him
   and dress him.
Most of all, he needs someone to love him and
   protect him.

But it isn't only babies who need love and
    attention.
We all need love and attention.
That is what families are all about.
Whether a family's members are young or old,
    they try to love and look after each other.

All human beings need the same things.
We all need food, warmth, clothing, and
    shelter to keep our bodies healthy.
And we all need love and care to keep our
    minds content.
Families try to meet all these needs in each
    other.

To meet these needs, each member of the
family has a part to play.
A man's part and a woman's part and a child's
part in a family are all different.
But sometimes one person must play two parts.

Have you ever been in a play at school and
played *two* small parts because there were
not enough people to go round?
Parts in families are sometimes rather like that.

Although all families try to fill the same needs,
   it would be wrong to say all families are
   alike.
Do you see why?

It is because the members of a family are
  different from house to house, from street
  to street.
And the parts they play in the family are
  different, too.

Look at the picture above.
You can see four houses next door to one
   another.

Let's see what sort of family lives in each
house, and how each family is different.

In the first house, Number 42, live Mrs. Fried,
her daughter Carol, and her granddaughter
Patsy.
As you can see, there are no men in the house.
That is because Mrs. Fried's husband died
recently, and because Carol is divorced from
her husband.

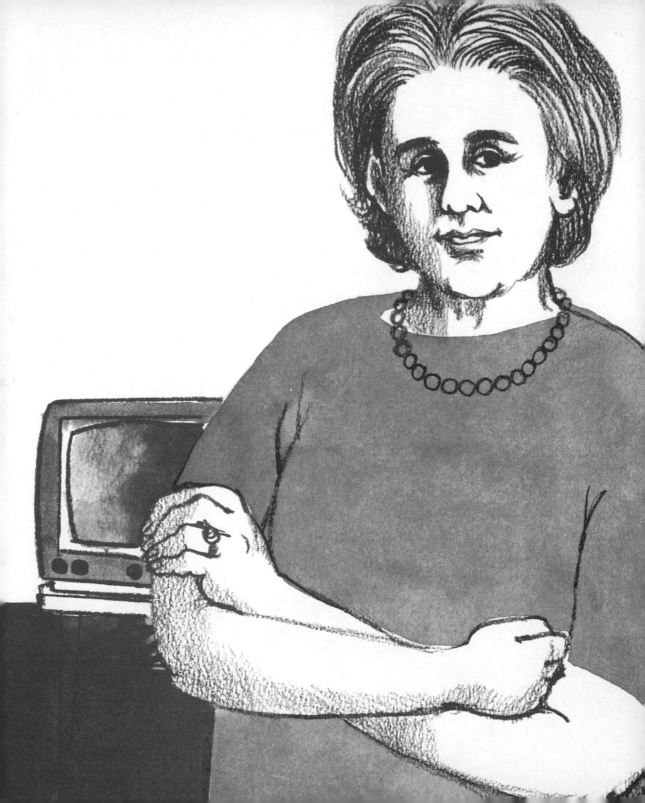

While Carol is out at work her mother takes
care of Patsy for her.

Because her husband is not living with them,
Carol has to try to be both a mother and a
father to Patsy.

So here you can see a family where one
woman must play two parts—her own and a
man's part.

If Carol marries again, Patsy will have a
stepfather.

Next door, in the house with the brown front
door, live Mr. and Mrs. Coppens and their
six children.

24

They need a lot of money each week to feed
and clothe everyone in the family.
To earn extra money, Mr. Coppens has to work
on weekends too.
This means that Mrs. Coppens must look after
her children without her husband's help
much of the time.
Her two oldest children help her look after
the younger ones.
So here you can see a family where the oldest
children must try to play extra parts, too.
They try to take care of the others in the
same way their father would.

Next door, in the white house, live four
    members of the Roberts family.
There are Mr. and Mrs. Roberts and their two
    children, Linda and John.
Linda and John were adopted by Mr. and Mrs.
    Roberts when they were babies.
They have grown up together.
Even though they are not related to their
    parents, John and Linda belong to the
    Roberts family.
So you can see that you do not have to be
    related to be part of a family.
Here you can see, too, that two adults can take
    on the part of parents by adopting children.

In the last house live Mr. and Mrs. Stanowsky.
They have just had their first baby.
While Mrs. Stanowsky feeds the baby, her
    husband is outside on a stepladder,
    painting the house.
In this house, Father is the member of the
    family who does the biggest jobs.
So here is a family where each member is
    playing one part.
There is a mother and there is a father, and
    they are not taking on extra parts.

So you see, there are many kinds of
  families.
But whatever the family is like, all the members
  depend on the others.
Someone has to earn money for the family to
  live on.
This person is sometimes called the
  breadwinner.

It may be Father or it may be Mother or it
  may be an older brother or sister.

Money has to come in to pay for rent, food, clothes, vacations, and many other things.

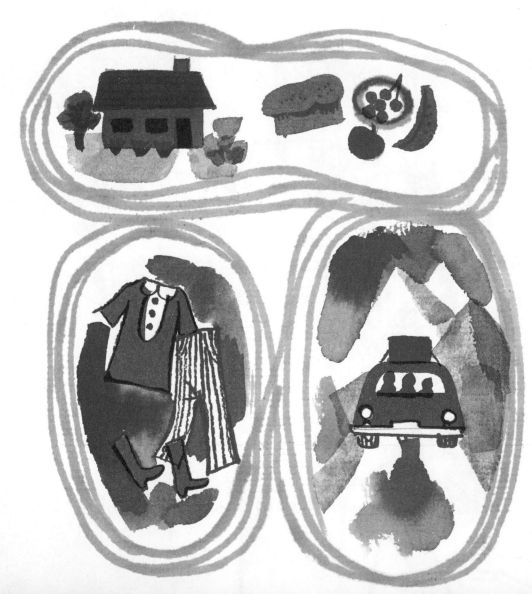

The breadwinner earns this money by working
in a store or an office or a factory or by
doing some other kind of job.

Usually one member of the family acts as
"mother."
It is often Mother herself, but it may be an
older sister, or even Father, if his wife has
died or they are divorced.
The "mother" of the family makes the home a
happy place to live in.
She cooks and sews, cleans and shops for
her family.

She is the one who makes you a
special cake on your birthday,
who wipes away your tears and
tells you a joke to make you
smile again when you are hurt.

Just as you depend on your family for many
  things, they too depend on you.
They depend on you to be kind to your friends
  and pets.
They depend on you to look both ways before
  crossing the street.
They depend on you not to tell lies or cheat at
  school.

The main job of parents is to help their
    children grow into capable, happy adults.
To do this, they make rules.
When you obey these rules you gain practice
    in obeying rules you will find in the world
    later on.

Most of the world is made up of families
   like yours in some ways.
By learning to live with and help your family,
   you are learning how most of the world lives.

famiglia Familia
FAMILIE famille
FAMILY

The word "family" includes lots of people
   besides your parents.
Can you think of some of the others?

The word "family" includes all your other
  relatives, too.
Your grandparents, aunts, uncles, cousins...

Some of your relatives may live nearby.
Others may live so far away you never see
them.

Perhaps on big holidays like Thanksgiving or
Christmas or Hanukkah the whole family
gets together.
You may play games and sing and chat, then
all sit down together to a big dinner with all
your favorite things.

When you are older, some of your happiest memories may be of times when your whole family was together.

ABOUT THE AUTHOR

Valerie Pitt was born and educated in England, and received a diploma in journalism from London Polytechnic. She has been a reporter on an English newspaper, a beauty and fashion writer on an English weekly magazine, and assistant fashion editor for *Woman's Own*, a magazine with a large circulation in England. She has traveled extensively in Europe and the United States, and has covered the Couture Collections in Florence and Rome.

She is now married and living in San Francisco. Among the other books she has written are *Let's Find Out About the City, Let's Find Out About Neighbors, Let's Find Out About Streets,* and *Let's Find Out About Clothes.*

ABOUT THE ARTIST

Gloria Kamen was born in New York City, attended school there, and studied at Pratt Institute, the Art Student's League, and the art school of the Brooklyn Museum.

She is married to a research chemist with the National Institute of Health at Bethesda, Maryland, and has three daughters.

She has received awards from the Educational Press Association of America for special educational features she has published. Traveling, cooking, hiking, and painting are her favorite pastimes.